Anywhere
but here

by Saxon Henry

sharktoothpress

Burden of Coincidence originally published in *Skidrow Penthouse*, Issue #2/Summer 1999.
Babylon originally published in the *New York Quarterly*, Issue 59/June 2003.
Tattered Visage originally published in *Dream of Venice*, Bella Figura Publications, December 2014.
Letter to Daedalus accepted for publication in a forthcoming issue of the New *York Quarterly*.

Published in the United States by Sharktooth Press, an imprint of
Rivershark Inc. Logomarks registered trademarks of Rivershark Inc.

Library of Congress Cataloging-in-Publication
Data Henry, Saxon. Anywhere But Here / Saxon Henry Trade Paperback
ISBN 978-0-9909507-4-5. Writer— New York (State)— New York— Poetry.

www.sharktoothpress.com

Cover design: Gerard McLean
Photo by Saxon Henry

v1.0_r2

For William Packard

.

I would like to thank Carmen Natschke with her astute editorial skills for being a second set of eyes and JoAnn Locktov for her expressive point of view regarding the sequencing of these poems.

Contents

I

Cartography

There are campfires burning
somewhere; the smoke
fills me with the desire to run.
I am built of vagabond stock—
nowhere is it written in the chart
mapping my genealogy,
only scribbled in my quest
to make my way my own.
A psychic told me,
"You're a phoenix;
you burn down lives
and arise from the ashes,
born anew."
In a field in France
a band of gypsies
dismantles a camp,
the urge
to burn some other ground
heeded once again.
I hear the sizzle,
the splatter of water
reducing flame to char;
feel the stamp
of hooves on clotted dirt,
the acrid air
all the horses need to know
of moving on.

Marking Time

We mark my father's
fifty-ninth year,
celebrate
that we were thrust
into a world of tight-lipped women
who beat their children
with their tongues.

The film heaves through
the camera's throat,
naming us, one by one,
like cracked and faded photographs
beyond our pasts,
our bruises hidden by repose—

Darkness Passing

1818. Lichened stone.
Mounded belly of grass.

You are the oldest piece of me
that I can find: You, reposed,
no longer able to rebel;
all backbone, hipbone
and grinning skull.

If words had spines,
this one I fondle, family,
would bow itself against my touch,
refusing to explain
why we have suffered so.

> *Are you the one who strives to touch me,*
> *who strains to push your dreams*
> *through the walls of weary night*
> *to prove I'm not the first to fear I'll die*
> *an unborn question?*

Resemblance

Where the slope buckles down the hollow,
the gnarled roots that tunnel the soil
remind me of the veins,
raised and rambling,
on the backs of Annie's hands.

I had scorned her old woman's skin,
worn thin from a lifetime
of tending skewed traditions.
The cook's apron she donned,
her perpetual chasuble,
was smudged with stains
where she'd wipe her hands of us
for being who we had to be.

Did she know
she hummed the song hunger sang—
mouthing my name—
during all those Sunday dinners?

All trees eventually fall
as the puny soil melts into
some runneling stream.
The steepest precipice erodes
as the world swallows itself,
unaware that its hunger
can never be assuaged.

The Haunting Moan of a Train's Passage

—for Karen Beam

I'm sleepless in my sister's guest room,
listening to the insistent cooing of a distant train
as it shuttles freight from one place to another
at breakneck speed.

My father's life is ebbing, though not as fast,
the clean air whirring from the oxygen tank
the only card he has left to play.
He is at war with the earthly plane
but he's tapped his daughters as adversaries,
forcing us to engage in skirmishes we did not choose,
yet again.

The ghosts of childhood and a mother, gone,
shuffle into the nursing home,
crowding into a corner near the hospital bed
to gape at the ensuing battle pitting a petulant child
against the women he conceived.

Though it is mortality he is facing down,
he cannot bear to admit we have no power
to save him from past sins.

The train's declaration, closer now, is a crooning—
the crisp air, dense with pale clusters of stars,
transporting its sonorous warning far.
Its meaning is explicit:
ignore me and death will pluck you
from these straight and narrow tracks
that trick your eye into believing they go on forever.

II

The Burden of Coincidence

—Lower Brule Reservation, South Dakota

I've been given a room where a bent fly swatter
and a Niobrara Cross on a beaded chain
hang on a nail by the dresser.
My window faces where Crazy Horse
and Iron Nation Streets converge—
a vacant corner since a housing project
was lifted from the soil. I watch
as children scatter, tossing fire crackers
onto the dirt. Each time I flinch
like my mother's poodle when he was smacked
for nervously chewing his own skin.

This hem of the prairie is splattered with light
punctuating the fourth of July. In the church next door,
the priest reads Psalms about the righteousness of giving
while the washing machines in the laundromat mouth
       Oh God.

Letter to Daedalus

How hurt you must have been
to see me plunging to the sea, bones
scrabbling air; a veil of feathers settling,
finally, to anoint my grave.

I've wanted to explain what would seem to you
so rash a thing. I did not mean
to worship movement,
but reverence is the only word
that could describe
how I treasured such freedom.

I didn't rise of my own volition.
The seraphs called me,
singing—*Holy, Holy, Holy*—
and I rushed toward them
knowing they stand closest to God;
forgetting they are born to be
perpetual flame. Father,
it was more than enough.

Ease

It is chaos behind the chipped stone wall,
the barbecue pit, the chain-link fence.
My yardman ignores the mass of vines
inching along the littered ground,
where animals crash through congealed brush.

My dogs, coddled in their pristine yard,
hunger to know this unruliness; envy all
who duck into the copious dust.

I was planting impatiens yesterday
in the flowerpot on the stone oven's lap
when I saw the deliberate procession:
red setter in back; black one in front,
a limp ginger cat swaying from his jaws.

Such ease only a mother should know
as she ferries her young through the world.

Abhayamudra*

Crashing toward moon
Ganesha's tusk understood
The loss in freedom.

*The gesture that banishes fear

Weather Report: November 4, 1995

I pull onto the highway
behind a chamois-colored van
with **Jesus Wept** pressed into its paint.

Sleet grazes the window;
cracks like ice in a glass
when water bites its frozen skin.
Yitzhak Rabin is shot in Tel Aviv.

This morning it was predicted
that nothing more than a few sprinkles
of light rain would fall.

Instrument

—For Min Tanaka,
Japanese Butoh Dancer

Your torso lisped
and the air faltered, altered—
driving body back to bone.
Movement's conduit,
Dionysian eyes,
you rendered stillness
helpless
as your sweat moved
the night to tears.

The Baptism of Daniel Martinez

——An article in the Santa Fe Reporter
celebrates prisoner Daniel's salvation.

The prisoners amble, two by two,
into the courtyard at dusk.
Facing the cattle tank,
each waits his turn to be submerged,
to have the jug of his body
fill with The Reverend's words
(which he imagines
will change each life forever).

Daniel steps into the tank.
The Reverend raises the handkerchief,
covers Daniel's nose and mouth—
       Be not afraid
he whispers,
taking Daniel down.

Cornet

—for Jim Ritter of Buck Creek Jazz Band

He blew the heart out of heaven,
flung the notes into the din
of man-made storm.
In three hours
he sifted through
all the cries
men were given
before the world
went sinfully silent.
He drew us in,
turned on the smokey room
and picked the ribs of noise
until sound bled—
moaning
          more, more.

Anywhere But Here

Monday morning, suburban diner—
all chrome and Olympic self-flattery.
Pink marble entombs a handful of people
who have the freedom but not the means
to be anywhere else.
A drunk, leaning over his plate,
lets his breakfast congeal
while he sips a Bloody Mary, half gone.

The television's tuned to the Travel Channel,
its screen tracking a single-engine plane
nosing its way through an African sky
the perfect imitation of cornflower blue.
When the cameraman cuts to a herd of rhinos
skirting around a lone giraffe, a smiling guide,
his pale vest blazing in the brutal light,
nods at oscillating Natives
who dance like their rhythm's inspired
by the whirring of the diner's blender.

A coin tumbling into the jukebox
awakens BB King and Clapton who croon
"Don't you know you're riding with the king?"
Swinging a leg to the beat of the song,
a woman who has dressed as if she isn't
past her prime chews a nail.
Suddenly she smiles like she's remembering
something she's sad she forgot.
Pretending to study the menu, she's hoping
to catch the drunk's eye.
He slips from the stool like he doesn't know this;
tossing change from his pocket onto the counter,
he nonchalantly passes her by.

On the TV, a lion lounging on beaten-down grass
is licking himself after a bloody meal
while an old man in a nearby booth is berating his wife
for her stupidity. The woman studies her lap
as the refined voice of the travel host drones on,
his insinuation almost lost in the grease-soaked air:
     you should be anywhere but here.

Near Puerto Limon

In Costa Rica, banana trees spill themselves
beneath the trestled tracks of trains.
Machetes rasp as cords are severed
and workers turn. Hooking fruit to wire,
they send it sailing.

Near Puerto Limon, a lizard clings
to the pitted screen
wrapped around the kitchen.
I've memorized his impotent smile,
the stern, unblinking candor
for which he has no lexicon.

Does he lie awake at night
as the woman next door
fills her backyard concrete sink
with unwashed bowls
or does he rest, unchanged,
while the plundered tree
still leans into its phantom weight?

June Oswald Watches Oliver Stone's J.F.K.

I try to relax as I take my seat.
I wish mama was here,
though I understand why she didn't come
even before the theater darkened
and daddy filled the screen.
I knew it was him, but only from pictures.
He's been gone so long there wasn't much else,
not even his voice until he yelled
      I am just a patsy.

The little girl jumps from the seat of her trike
and bounds into daddy's open arms.
I've seen her before in photographs
pressed into the tattered album
secretly slid beneath my bed.
There's mama: younger, smiling,
not as stooped as she is now.
How I wish everyone knew
our lives had also been brutalized
by that damned rifle's blasphemy.

Could it have been daddy with his reckless passion
and the stunted limitation of his anger
who watched intently as the car slid down the peopled street?
Is it possible that this man who said he loved me
steadied that shining auburn mane
in the crosshairs of that scope?
How I wish I had the answers
as the actor raised the barrel, again.
Again, the gun's report; Jackie reaching.

Babylon

"Fallen, fallen is Babylon the Great!
…God has remembered her iniquities…
…mix a double draught for her in the cup she mixed…"
Revelations 18

The wind lifts spray from a lit fountain above
a gouged bench on a platform for the 1 and 9
where raucous girls, one with orange matted hair
and a ditzy brunette in a poodle coat,
disregard stares and laughter.
Farther downtown, an anxious woman in a fur
watches the board at Penn Station
while her escort checks his watch again,
as if his need for a hit of culture has been sated
by the evening's operatic rush and voluminous meal.
When they board the express train for Babylon
do they return to an avenue of brick houses
poised on the brink of the Great South Bay?
As they careen from the tunnel into the vaulted language of night,
how intently will they stare out the window, silent as sentinels?

Tattered Visage

—Personifying an architectural detail
near Venice's Accademia Bridge

I would tremble if I could;
rant, rave, slink myself
into the effluvia
that drowns the watery world
eating away at my vision.

I choke on the cries
that would wake them up—
capricious, gawking masses
fixing their stares
on this tattered visage.

They are drawn to me, even as
they recoil, aping as they peer
into my soul exposed by loathsome time.
As if they could mimic my pain!
As if they've could abide such numb panic!

It's an agony to watch: not me;
them—the flotsam expecting
the Accademia Bridge. They turn to me
instead and I witness their terror.
I stare; they cringe.

It's my fear-struck mask
that rankles—my eyes frozen in fright,
tongue wagging at the elemental torture
devouring me from the outside in.
I AM Venezia, its dream crumbling.

Matthew Barney at the Guggenheim

It took him eight years
to discover whether he had the balls
to flaunt his manhood.
Rebellion is rarely discrete:
lines of rubber laid down on asphalt,
a fist tossed through the teeth
of the fucker who fakes a dare.
Was it the murky slide of birth
that made him obsessed with death,
the ice-clear bustier trailing off
to an umbilical cord
wrapped around his feet a clue?
I study each artifact he presented
and I am at a loss to decide
whether life is imitating art
or the other way around.
Piles of potatoes decomposing,
opaque stains on a pristine page,
make me want to scream,

Would someone play
that goddamned piano?

But silence keeps ticking on
like a mute metronome
berating the footfalls
echoing from the rotunda floor
for their uninspired drudgery.
And Barney's message gags
on its own creation
amidst such rampant deconstruction.
Only the lamb appears as innocent
as I need it to be—
eyes gone to slits of resignation,
heart plundered,
no cry left in its truant lungs.

The Paradise of Sadness

—from "A Season in Hell" by Arthur Rimbaud

The light on the still water of the lake
charms the eye. The first touch
of yellow has burgeoned on the limb
as I listen to the scattered warble of the birds.
The cleft in the tree that beckons them home
will become a trap when the crows move in.

Natural enemies. Prolific ferocity.
Safety's illusion. The death pose of road kill:
the curved body of the squirrel
curled on its side on the painted line
imitating gentle rest.
Swift lull. Slumber. Pitch of night.

We list toward the dark sea of death
in this paradise of sadness.
"What will I do for a cape?"
Susie asks her son on Halloween.
"Let your darkness be your cloak," he replies.

How will the darkness find us?
On the roadbed, flat on the back, reaching skyward,
eyes dazed as they mirror the soft glow
of a dusk-laden sky;
or turned on the side like a baby in the womb?
They role the footage for the hundredth time.
I watch the floors pancake, the dust rise,
the paper drift rhythmically earthward.
What would those ghosts birthed on 9/11,
now parading down Manhattan's altered canyons,
have us believe about living?

Triangulation

Through the unknown, remembered gate
When the last of earth left to discover
Is that which was the beginning. —*T.S. Eliot*

Ascending through this lofty landscape,
I try to imagine the first scribe
to explain the jagged terrain to a blank page—
not a wordy turning of the slopes I see,
clotted with silvery sage, into a narrative arc,
but a plotted pastiche in fluctuating relief.
The explicitness of the cartographer's art
manifests wavering lines
exploding into whorls of density
as they describe the pinnacles
whose reflections slide across my windshield.

Mapmaking's resistance to extravagance
condemns surveyors to brevity,
arming early topographers with little more than
transit, compass, sextant and caliper.
"Explain how high the craggy mountains loom,
and only where they begin and end,"
the instruments warn.
"Leave it to the poets to convey
the sentience of sienna foothills
pocked with plumes of mesquite,
and the loneliness of a lozenge-shaped lake,
its ashen ruffle of a silt-laden edge
bone-dry in its need."

I breach Rabbit Ears Pass on this wet spring day
two centuries after explorers as cunning as
Frémont, Long and King indexed these summits.
Water rushes through each crevice

as if directed by a symphony of cues,
spilling itself into overflowing springs
saturating each sloping quagmire I see.
The trees have not yet leafed this high,
a world in which the air remains so chilled
smudges of snow linger in snatches of shade.

When America's first voyagers
reached this exalted altitude,
no coherent passage had been drilled
near the boulders shaped like the pointed ears
that gave the peak its name.
I salute them as I eclipse the cut,
now an essential scar,
and notice Lake Catamount
resting so far below its surface glints
like a blue-green marble catching the late-day light.
As I make my way to Steamboat Springs,
the highway dictates that I descend
into a flat expanse a geographer of long ago
declared the Yampa Valley.

This trek from Denver
has consumed most of an afternoon—
a sojourn that would have claimed large swaths
of a westward-bound adventurer's life,
his days spent triangulating
the tectonic secrets he craved.
Did he realize his sickle mimicked the pulse of time
as the crescent of his blade
whispered to the sagebrush?
Did he know each thwack of a hatchet
striking conifer after conifer
brought him closer to a precipice
being anointed with his name?

Once above the timberline,
loose rocks skittering beneath his feet,
was he calm as he positioned his tripod,
fitting its cradle with the eloquent alidade,
knowing he would be the first to map
the incomprehensible views
dwarfing his anatomy?

His pupils would have swelled
as he squinted to align the peaks,
calculating enormous chasms
he was finally ready to explain.
Was the great muscle of his heart
thumping as he relished
the genius of his instruments
at concretizing the heights
to which the Rockies soar?
Did he later take pleasure
in the scriber's swiveling
as it nimbly portrayed
a visual of the dark hollows
it had taken him hours to traverse?
Or was he simply not the ilk of man
to be enthralled,
even as he set the range-pole
on a place I travel through,
no longer mysterious as a consequence
of the single-mindedness of his precision?

He Sprang Like Ore from the Silence of Stone

—Rainer Maria Rilke, Sonnets to Orpheus

I stayed two weeks in the nether world
with a man who'd lived in a house unlivable.
He sprang like ore from the silence of stone,
I from the sedge by the river.

I wanted a silent stone to speak.

But if he had burned to whisper,
I would have turned, like Orpheus,
who watched Eurydice fade away.
And he could no more speak
than I could keep from turning.

SAXON HENRY

III

Wanderlust

It's 3 a.m.
and the sky is weeping light.
The wandering Leonids
are streaking across
this slice of darkness.
I beg daylight not to mask
the magic, but of course it comes.
Then I remember: though invisible,
those meteors still glance overhead,
mimicking how you dream
of getting lost.

I imagine letting you walk
through the pale alone.
My heart holds,
but only for a moment.
Then I return to my own dream:
you—the last naked nomad—
sauntering toward my bed
while the meteors speed and burn,
stunned to find themselves
indistinguishable from
the shimmering, sun-soaked air.

Now Hiring Night Cooks

Seen on a restaurant marquis

He would have to have
the passion of a troubadour,
the palette of Van Gogh,
the fire of Prometheus,
the courage of a god,
hands that could kneed wistful wonder
from the pulsing sex of dawn,
a mouth unafraid
to suck the color from evening's dusky sky,
the audacity to marvel at what he's doing
as he unflinchingly drops the heavens
into the dizzy heat
of a skillet as large as the moon.

Who has the nerve to braise the night;
to garnish it with a prayer moaned
between clinched teeth?

Tell me, who?

Deciding to Depart

You stretched out on the bed
like a teen god in your blue jeans
and tee shirt. All the lost decades
cascaded forward in my fierce hunger
to be sanctified—a reverence
that only boys and girls
are astonished enough to comprehend.
We drank coffee, recited Frank O'Hara,
listened as Morrison crooned
the room past silence.
I sat, bare-assed and wanting,
as you held sway over my need.
When you read "To the Harbormaster"
in the winnowed light of the afternoon,
I swallowed the throb that swelled in me.
"...I am always tying up
and then deciding to depart..."
                              you read,
and my own restless hull
convulsed with the need to anchor.

I can't remember why
I gave up on the girl
who went missing from my youth,
the curving lisps of her hips and breasts
now a dream. I've learned so little
about the tying up;
so much about the departing.

For Lolita

Please, lover, imagine me:
the warm coil of feeling
that will wake you in the quickening night;
the damp on your brow,
the whimper rushing from your lips.
I shall not exist
if you do not imagine me
awakening you to keen desire
with a whispered plea:
> *please, lover, imagine me.*

Cloud Busting

candlelight,
midnight sheets,
tiny cove
in lashing seas,
skin—that skin—
heat, heart,
appetite:
fill me.
sonorous sounding,
surfacing: no!
I won't
give
you back.
that cock—
my quiver—
homebound,
crashing,
stunned by flight.
drift, dear.
breast like moon
rests in sky
of strong chest.
breath, memento,
love leaking
down these thighs;
stir, rustle, turn—
"let me wrap myself
around this beauty."
I was born to rest
in that embrace.

Art:History

Who would find me in this life I have created
assuming someone else's falsities:

the jackal-headed god who plucks at the chain
as they weigh my heart against the feather of truth; you—

wishing to place the unhasped necklace around my throat, believing
that the pavé diamonds will disguise your cross's proclivity?

In the Sistine Chapel, God commands Eve to stand upright,
while above her head she participates in The Fall of Man.

And below, Adam reclines—one hand extended
toward the reach of God's articulate finger.

Knife Sharpening

There's a rhythm to sharpening knives;
my ex-husband knew it well.
He would grab them one by one
and take them through their scales.
Their metal has a rawness
the other utensils lack.
The edges boasting keenness
and a gentle tapering back.
The thick ones sounded resonant,
the stubby ones flat;
the long and slender blades
like the yowls of testy cats.
He would flip them
through their motions
every Sunday afternoon,
never deigning to notice
spiky fork or curvy spoon.
The tube of gritty diamonds
took on a demented ring
as he coaxed the sound from its throat,
making its roughness sing.

I steered clear of the knife-block—
for hours, my notice discreet—
as it took those blades quite some time
to cool from the dexterous heat.
I taught myself the method
once we had divorced.
The only challenge I couldn't achieve:
to plant them in my own back with force.

IV

Mythical Models for Twenty-First-Century Wives

Daphne

I was frozen at first, afraid to move.
Splinters fester, you know.
If one invaded my taut skin,
who would remove its dark heart?
So, from the start it was too late.
I was already thinking, lost,
as wooden as the bed frame we'd bought
the week before the wedding.

Persephone

My marriage is hell. No, really.
A difficult address for a precocious girl
who once delighted in the profusion of hibiscus—
those yellow tongues protruding
toward the clamor of bees.

In early Spring, when Japonica pushes
her passion-tinted blooms from icy stems,
my husband puts on his dark mask of longing.
It's always a fight. But I have no choice
but to rise like that one dry, restless leaf
remaining from autumn,
made nervous by the wind.

He could never live like this: baffled
like the butterfly that stubbornly fidgets
outside the plate glass window,
confounded by the invisible wall
of unattainable sky.

Exploring the Voice of Paul Gauguin

Mette, my dear husbandless wife,
have you heard what they are saying?
So I have savage blood—don't we all:
just look at the curse of Original Sin
ravaging Eve before The Fall.
I have this awkward involvement with her,
it is true; both mother-protector
and mother-seducer. But I am tiring
of my quest to redeem her. And, Mette,
the night silence permeates my being;
the arsenic waits.

You will take comfort in these admissions,
I am sure, for I am destroying my fantasies
the further I enter into them, despising so
my own reality. I have tried to trust;
tried to unleash my impotent passion,
but I have so little confidence. Ah, Mette,
remember when I said,

>*Faith and Love are Oxygen.*
>*They alone sustain life?*

Is it any wonder the arsenic waits;
I cannot breathe.

Posturing in the Piazza del Duomo

Traipsing across the tail
of Victor Emmanuel's rearing horse,
a pigeon performs its intrinsic dance
in the shadow of the Duomo di Milano.
Reflecting upon his zeal
are theologians and kings
telescoped on spires,
so grandly foisted above
the ornate façade,
the bird is but a speck.
The pigeon thinks nothing
of their lauded elevation,
captivated as he is
by his own stealthy move
to the ruffled mane of a stately lion
lounging below the king.
A crusade is on the pigeon's mind
as he traverses the cat's pillowed paw
draped across the shield
nestled to its beastly breast,
though his campaign is far from political.
He expects his stubborn strutting
will attract a particular lady's gaze—
this latest sortie moving him closer
to her perch atop the lion's nose,
its flared nostrils a petite plateau
with room enough for her alone.

As I count the anointed hands
reaching into the vivid sky,
I wager not one of these
pious princes of the realm
would have flexed a middling muscle
to acknowledge this scourge
of the avian species.

I despise them, too,
so I blame my notice of the winged waifs
on an exhibition celebrating
the genius of Leonardo da Vinci
I had contemplated all afternoon.
The artist was known for buying birds
he found caged in market stalls
and promptly setting them free.
Did he liberate these nuisances of modernity
as ardently as he freed
ducks, geese, woodcocks and quail?
It is far from the unfledged I observe
as I follow the female fluttering
to the lion's haunch,
a maneuver swiftly mimicked
by her obstinate admirer.

As evening bathes the stone church
in a sensual glow,
I have to give him credit
for refusing to acknowledge defeat—
blindly bobbing along the muscled thigh
as she expeditiously flaps away.
Twilight's exuberance
frenzies his efforts to track her.
Caring little that his attempts to copulate
are gaining little ground,
he bounces on and on and on.
Will he pause as night falls,
resuming his advances in her direction
once morning's light glances across
the righteous faces
of Milano's decorative deities?

Or will he choose another conquest
as the bells peal
to announce the advent of a new day?
The object of his fascination
beside the point,
he will be there, inflating his breast
and twirling just as fancifully,
the curse of his DNA
sentencing him to the grandiose lust
he is hard-wired to obey.

Variations on a Theme: For a Gay Friend Coming Out

for David

This poem wants to be about the you I knew—
bent over a guitar grabbing after bits of noise
and crescendo.

How hard we laughed when you rushed for the plane,
banging that old guitar case
on the half-glassed doors,
such nervous joy on your face!
You turned to wave but your hands were full.
Mine lifted spontaneously,
fingers fretting with the air
as you stumbled up the narrow stairs
toward a new life you hoped would satisfy
a you I might not recognize
as I write this, months later.

Inspired by the Peruvian lilies on the table,
ubiquitous in restaurants for their renowned longevity,
this poem wants to know
if you're still strumming some melody,
somewhere;
or if in your rush to make up for lost time,
you forgot how silence, not applause,
follows a song's imperfect cadence.

An Exploration of Attachment

Spring

I dream that I am crippled;
crawling over rocks
and fallen trees.

Someone bends and whispers
you're not going to like this;
lifts me and carries me
to even ground.

Summer

How long it must have taken her:
scurrying from limb to limb
weaving pungent greenery.
Yesterday she tossed it
from the sycamore tree—

once supple and compliant; now
dried husks crumbling.

Autumn

I watch him feed the geese
as the fallen leaves rattle down
the driveway's spine.

He thinks if they are sated
they will stay. But once again
they each take wing;
lift, dripping, from the pond
and search the far horizon.

Winter

The hawk flattens her belly;
braces for the heft
of an icy current:
  felt, though never seen.

Spring

The cicada's scavenged hull
clings to the woody stalk.

I awaken to the cricket's call:
unfettered rubbing—
indulgent declaration.

Girl in Combat

So much early nonsense
always to explain,
shifts like heavy metal
sifting through my brain.

I'm a girl in battle.
The skirmish is so sweet.
Watch me score the knockout;
watch these dancing feet.

I turned in my stilettos
for a pair of mary janes
in protest of the gown ups—
wisdom's their refrain.

Turns out the shoes don't matter;
it's what's inside your head.
The thought of those five-inch heels
still fills me with dread.

A pair of boots across the room—
heaviness so clear.
Will they end up on my feet,
bringing combat near?

What do the boys remember?
What do they soon forget?
Their toys left on the playground
into these boots they step.

Couldn't I forget myself—
the femme and the sweet;
Crush whatever crossed my path
stomping down the street?

These boots: they feel so raucous
like a curbside fight in June—
sweat pouring from bodies,
blood gushing, toothy wounds.

If I set things in motion—
a maniac with a plan—
I'd beat up everyone I'd meet,
make that everyone I can!

But it's not my disposition
regardless of my shoes.
And, I'd just use all my make-up
hiding cut, gash and bruise.

Girl I am for certain:
it's a simple truth.
Just as the clothes don't make the man,
my shoes can be uncouth.

Reared in the age of sock hops
when shoes had little say,
I don't need to cover my feet
to dance the night away.

Plume

It is difficult
to face
someone else's struggle
when it stokes the fire
of your own
painful burning,
especially when
you've labored for years
to swallow the smoke.

www.ingramcontent.com/pod-product-compliance
Lightning Source LLC
Chambersburg PA
CBHW071104040426
42443CB00013B/3396